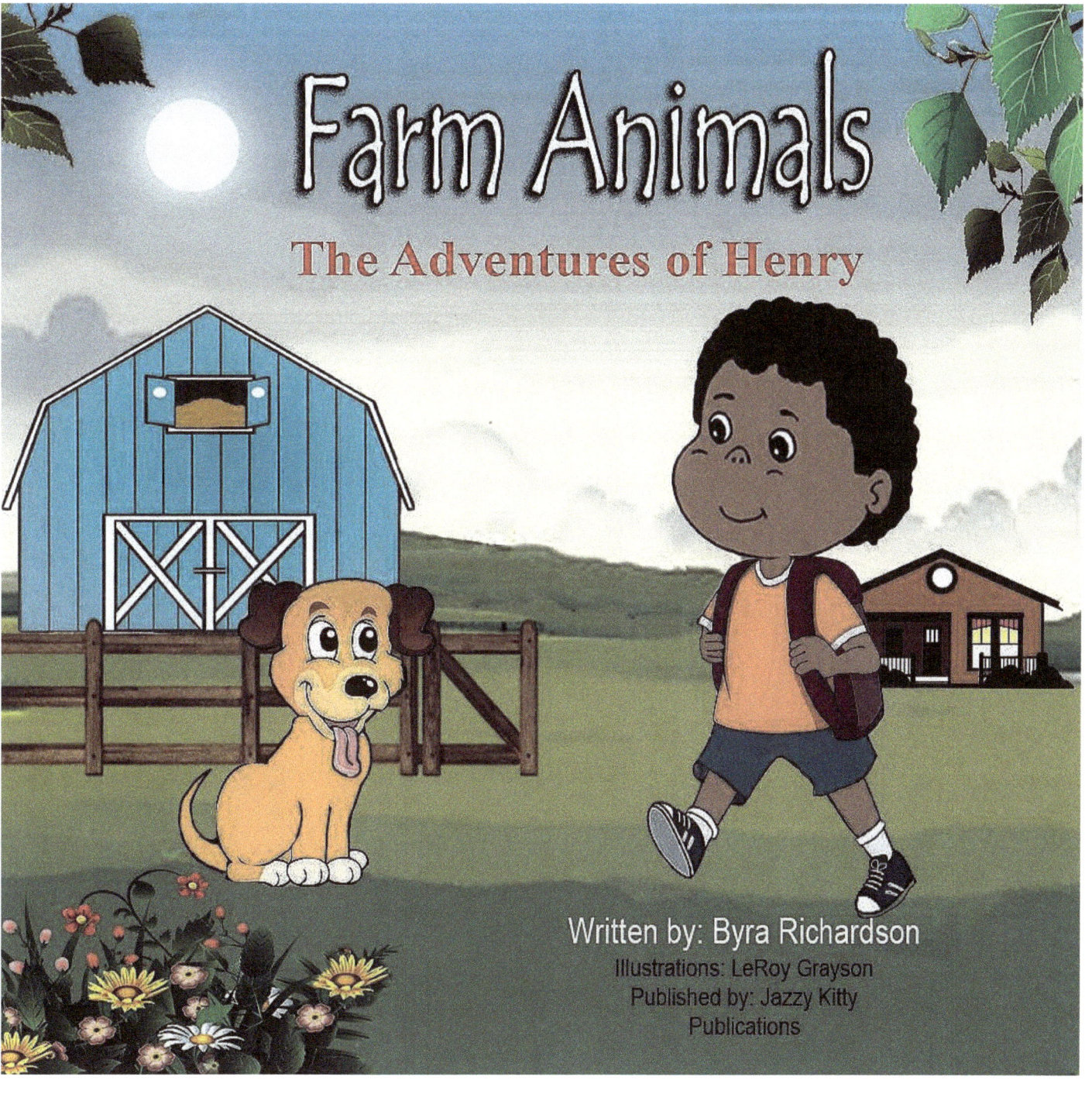

A Fictional Story

THE ADVENTURES OF HENRY

FARM ANIMALS

BY BYRA RICHARDSON

Illustrations by Leroy Grayson

Little Henry

Little Henry is heading to the farm to see a blue barn with yellow yarn.

While at the farm Little Henry saw a farmer who works with a hammer.

Little Henry also saw at the farm a brown chicken who moved with a quicken!

While at the farm Little Henry

also saw

A Goat who wore a purple coat.

Little Henry also saw at the farm

a black horse

Who was very short.

While at the farm Little Henry

also saw

a pink pig who wore a yellow wig.

Little Henry also saw at the farm

a yellow duck

who happens to be stuck.

While at the farm Little Henry

also saw

a llama who was with his mama.

Little Henry also saw at the farm a sheep that like to peep.

While at the farm Little Henry

also saw

a cow who had a friend

called Owl.

Little Henry also saw at the farm a black dog that stood on a log.

While at the farm Little Henry

also saw by chance

a horse who loves to dance

Little Henry also saw at the farm a hen who carried a pen.

While leaving the farm, Little Henry asked the farmer can he use his phone to call his mother for a car ride home.

The End

The Adventures of Henry Farm Animals is a children's book for educational purposes.

This book helps children use their literacy and cognitive thinking and learn through play.

This book is very amusing to each child whose ready to take an adventure with Henry to a farm!

A special thank you to my family and friends for all the words of encouragement through this journey.

Thanks to my publisher and illustrator, who helped me bring my vision to life.

And to my support team, just know that you all are awesome, and I appreciate everyone who has stood by my side.

The Adventures of Henry Farm Animals

By Byra Richardson

Illustrations by Leroy Grayson

Editor: Anelda Attaway

Published by Jazzy Kitty Publications

Wil, DE 19720

877.782.5550 - http://www.jazzykittypublications.com

anelda@jazzykittypublications.com

Copyright © 2022 Byra Richardson

ISBN 978-1-954425-42-2

Library of Congress Control Number: 2022901312

Credits: Book Cover, image and illustrations by Leroy Grayson of Quality Pictures qualitypictures2@aol.com; Book Editing by Anelda Attaway Co-editor Leroy Grayson; Logo Designs by Andre M. Saunders and Jess Zimmerman.

All rights are explicitly reserved worldwide. This book is protected under the copyright laws of the United States of America. This book may not be copied or reprinted for commercial profit or net income. The purpose of short quotations or occasional page copying for personal or group study is permitted and promoted. Permission to copy will be freely granted upon request for Worldwide Distribution. Printed and published in the United States of America. Created Jazzy Kitty Greetings Marketing & Publishing, LLC dba Jazzy Kitty Publications are utilizing Microsoft Publishing and BookCoverly Software.

DRAW A LINE TO MATCH THE FARM ANIMALS

www.ingramcontent.com/pod-product-compliance
Lightning Source LLC
Chambersburg PA
CBHW040001290426
43673CB00077B/301